Dad

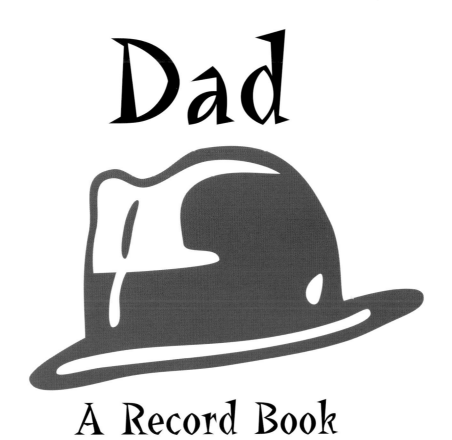

A Record Book

© 1998 Havoc Publishing

ISBN 1-57977-116-5

Published and created by Havoc Publishing

San Diego, California

First Printing, January 1998

Designed by Juddesign

Made in China

Please write to us for more information on our

Havoc Publishing Record Books and Products.

HAVOC PUBLISHING

6330 Nancy Ridge Drive, Suite 104

San Diego, California 92121

Contents

All About Me

Name _____

Birth date _____

My description _____

_____

_____

_____

_____

Where I grew up _____

_____

_____

_____

_____

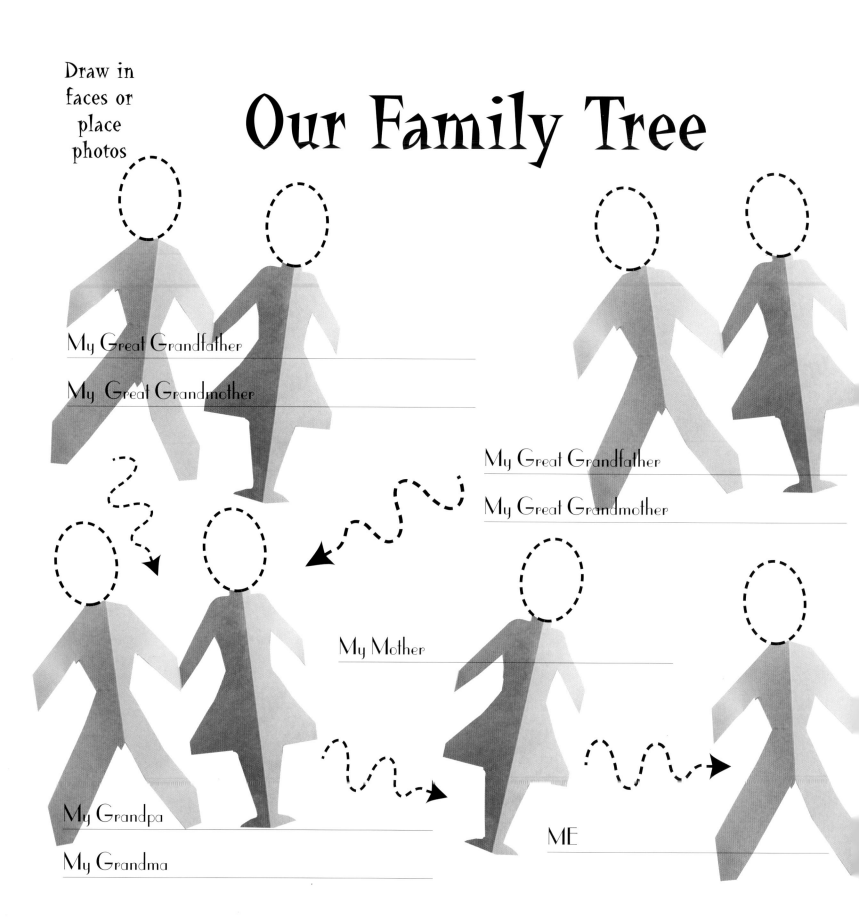

Draw in faces or place photos

Our Family Tree

My Great Grandfather

My Great Grandmother

My Great Grandfather

My Great Grandmother

My Mother

My Grandpa

My Grandma

ME

My Great Grandmother

My Great Grandfather

My Great Grandfather

My Great Grandmother

My Grandmother

My Grandfather

My Father

Dad's Side

Family History

Photo

Photo

Photo

Photo

Nationality of my family

Some interesting facts

Family stories handed down

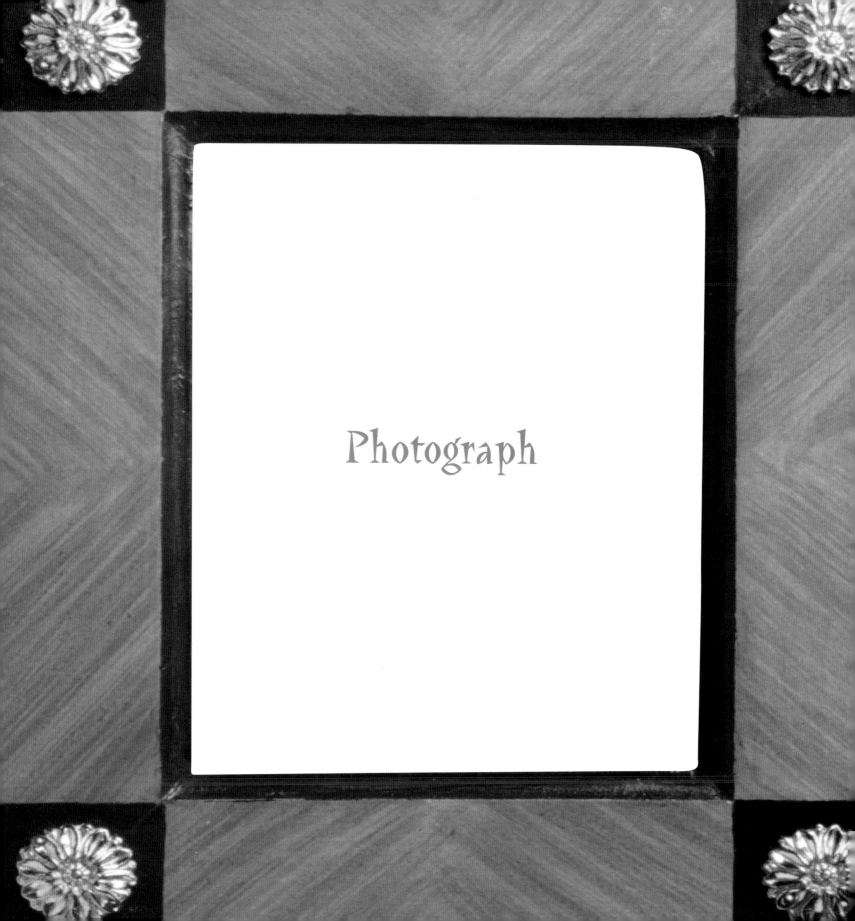

Photograph

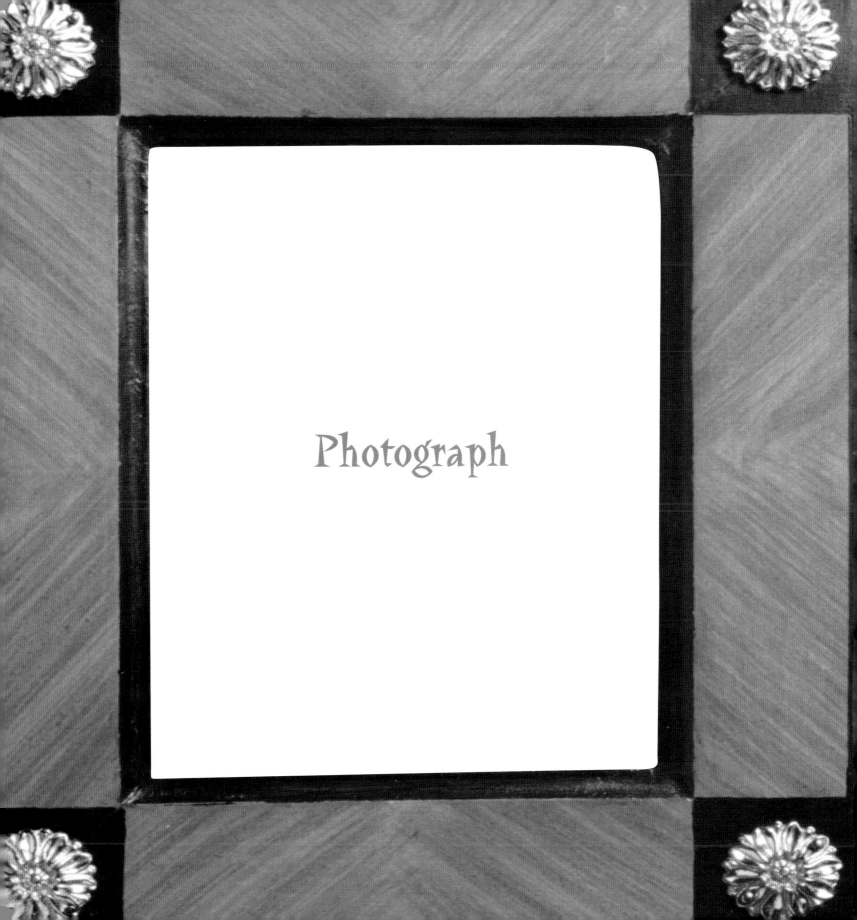

Photograph

The Early Years

My earliest memories

_____

_____

_____

_____

About my room

_____

_____

_____

About my neighborhood

_____

_____

_____

My hobbies
& interests

_____

_____

_____

Favorite birthdays

_____

_____

_____

_____

Favorite childhood memories

_____

_____

_____

Most exciting sports event I ever attended

_____

_____

Most exciting sports event I ever participated in

_____

_____

My Childhood Favorites

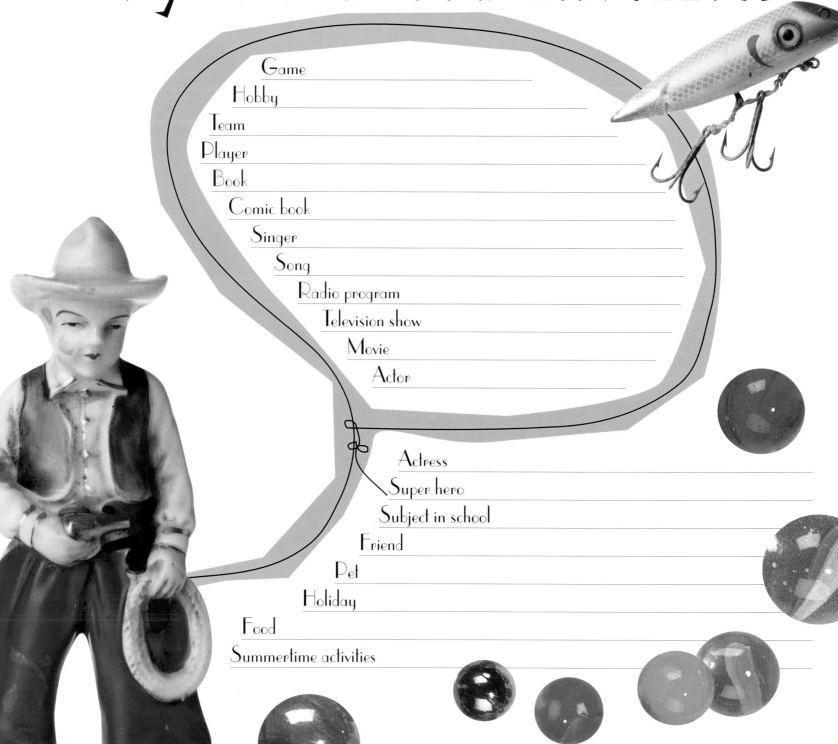

Game _____

Hobby _____

Team _____

Player _____

Book _____

Comic book _____

Singer _____

Song _____

Radio program _____

Television show _____

Movie _____

Actor _____

Actress _____

Super hero _____

Subject in school _____

Friend _____

Pet _____

Holiday _____

Food _____

Summertime activities _____

What the World was Like

World leaders
_____

_____

Famous scandals
_____

_____

International issues
_____

_____

National issues
_____

_____

Local issues
_____

_____

Famous movie stars
_____

_____

When I was Growing Up

A postage stamp cost _____

A candy bar cost _____

A gallon of gas cost _____

A loaf of bread cost _____

A movie ticket cost _____

An ice cream cost _____

A haircut cost _____

A gallon of milk cost _____

Events that dramatically changed my life _____

_____

_____

_____

School Days

Schools attended

Graduation

Funniest school story

The best class ever

My favorite subject

Favorite & memorable teachers

After school . . .

Sports I played

Clubs and Activities

School friends

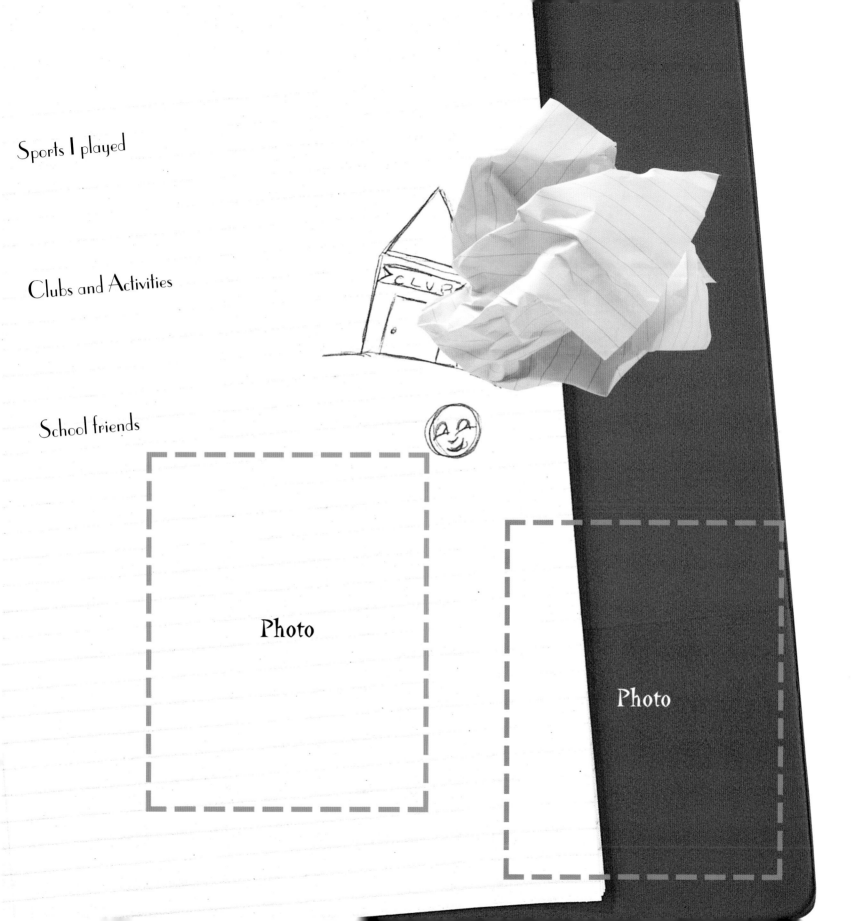

Photo

Photo

Photograph

The Gang

My earliest friendships

_____

_____

_____

Where we hung out

_____

Funniest story

_____

_____

Pranks

_____

_____

_____

My friends now
_____
_____
_____
_____

How we met
_____
_____
_____

Stories about our friendship
_____
_____
_____
_____
_____
_____
_____

Photograph

Clothes I wore

_____

_____

_____

Trends & fads I followed

_____

_____

_____

My most unusual hair style

_____

_____

What I did for entertainment & fun

_____

_____

_____

_____

_____

A Sign of the Times

DRIVER LICENSE

DMV DMV

Class: C

EXPIRES DOB'01

Photo

Year I got my driver's license

What type of car I drive

How many miles I've driven

The Wheels

Getting my driver's license

Cars I wanted

Photo of first car here

My first car
_____

First car I purchased & how much I paid
_____

Others cars I've had
_____

My dream cars
_____

_____

Memorable car story
_____

_____

_____

_____

Photo

On the Job

My very first job

My first full-time job

Job I liked the most

My occupation

The most important promotion

The most challenging job

The best career decision

Goals

Photo

Career
_____
_____
_____

Family
_____
_____
_____

Health
_____
_____
_____

About Mom

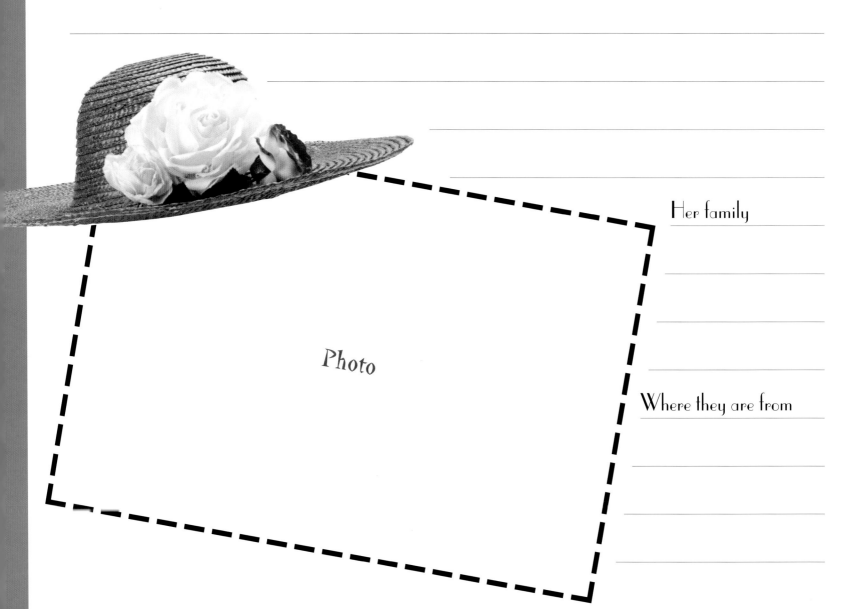

When & how I met your mom

Her family

Where they are from

Photo

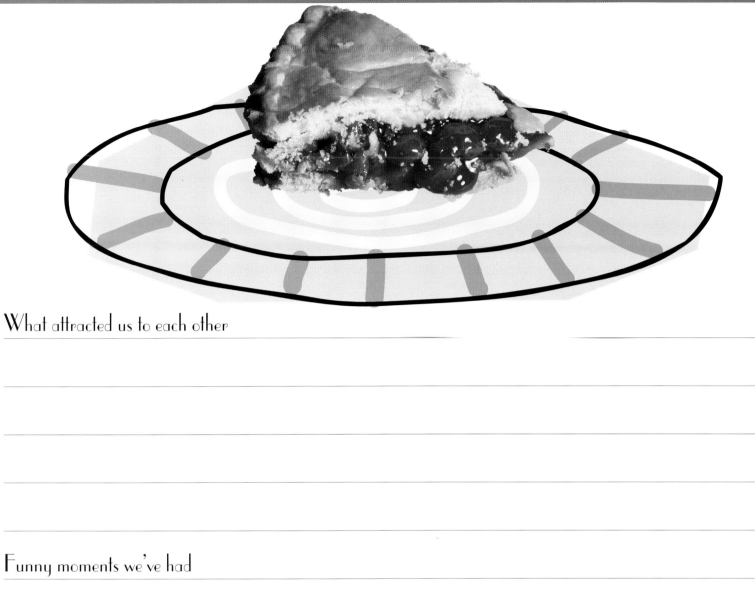

What attracted us to each other

Funny moments we've had

Mom quirks

The Proposal

Date

Place

How I proposed

Her reaction

Wedding Bells

Date & time

_____

Ceremony location

_____

Reception location

_____

The weather that day

_____

Special people that attended

_____

_____

My favorite wedding day memory

_____

_____

_____

We honeymooned at

_____

_____

_____

_____

Photograph

Photograph

I'm a Father!

Your birth date

Your birth place

Your full name

What it means & why we chose it

What I was doing when you decided to arrive

My first reaction to you

I still laugh when I think about

As a father I try to be

My proudest moment as a father

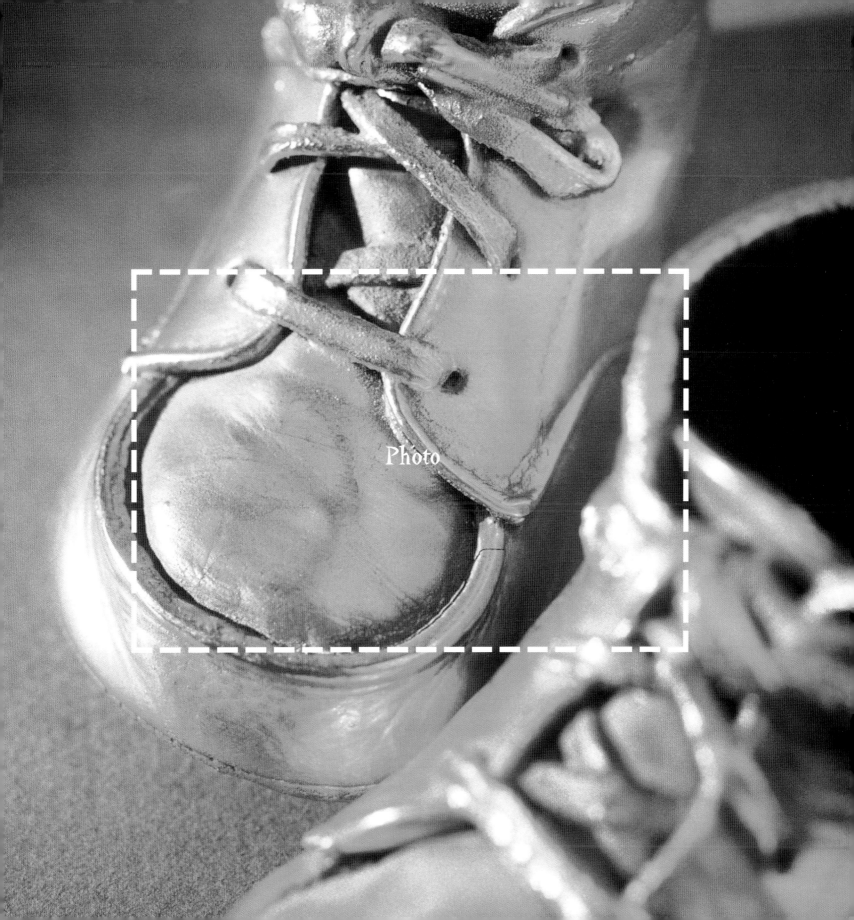

Photo

Let's Talk Shop

My best creation _____

_____

_____

My worst creation _____

_____

_____

I enjoyed teaching you about _____

_____

_____

_____

Tools I use most often & why

I was proud of the time I

Photograph

Photograph

Photo

Dad-isms

What I enjoy doing with you

_____

_____

_____

We always

_____

_____

_____

Best memories together

_____

_____

_____

Things I always say to you

_____

_____

_____

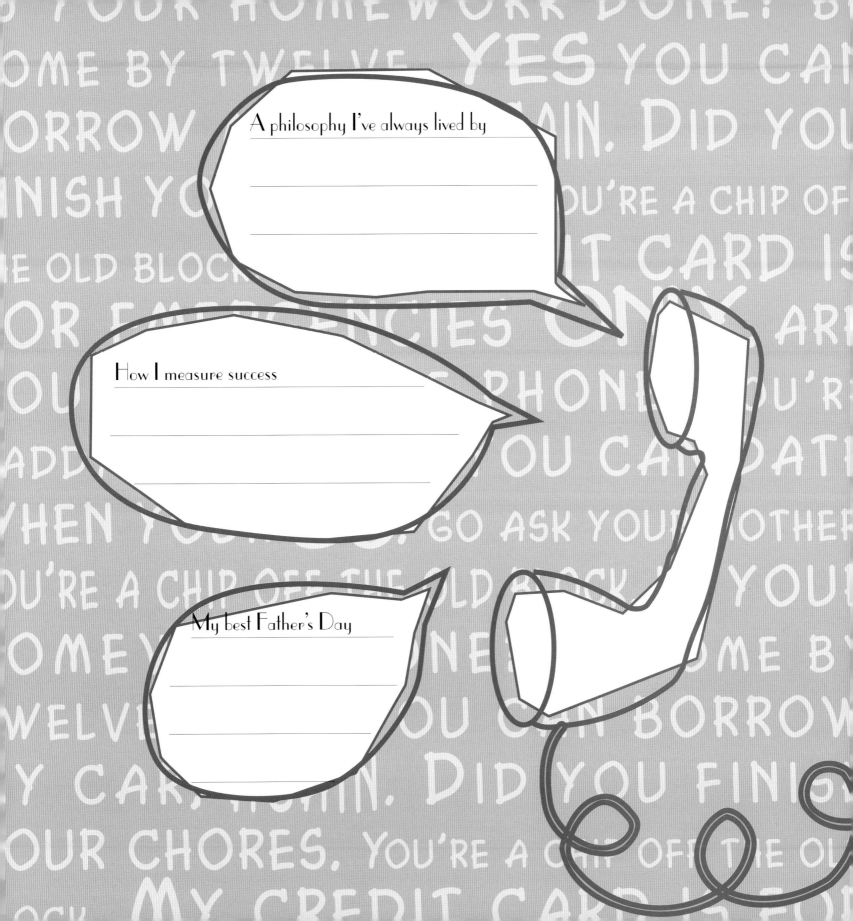

A philosophy I've always lived by

_____

_____

_____

How I measure success

_____

_____

_____

My best Father's Day

_____

_____

Family Celebrations . . .

Birthdays

_____

_____

_____

_____

Favorite things we celebrate

_____

_____

_____

_____

Special events

_____

_____

_____

_____

Events & Traditions

My favorite family recipe

Holidays
_____

_____

Traditions
_____

_____

_____

Get-togethers
_____

_____

_____

_____

Ingredients
_____

Directions
_____

_____

_____

_____

_____

Changes I've Seen

Computers

_____

_____

Technology

_____

_____

Politics

_____

_____

Media

_____

Modern Technology

Inventions during my lifetime

_____

_____

_____

Firsts I've experienced

_____

_____

_____

Greatest invention of my time

_____

_____

_____

Invention that had the most impact on my life

_____

_____

The TRAVELER in Me

The most memorable trip
_____
_____
_____

People I've met along the way
_____
_____

Favorite road trip
_____

The most exciting trip
_____
_____
_____

The most boring trip
_____
_____
_____

Different places I've been
_____
_____
_____

My favorite getaways
_____
_____
_____

The most exotic place I've been
_____
_____

Photograph

Photograph

My Style

Favorite casual attire _____

_____

Favorite business attire _____

_____

Favorite special occasion attire _____

_____

Favorite ties _____

_____

Attitude in life _____

_____

What I do to relax _____

_____

❏ This is definitely my style.
❏ I wouldn't be caught dead in this.

❏ This is definitely my style.
❏ I wouldn't be caught dead in this.

❏ This is definitely my style.
❏ I wouldn't be caught dead in this.

Some Thoughts...

Item I got rid of years ago that I still wish I had
_____

_____

The best advice I've received
_____

_____

_____

If I could choose one _____

Quote to pass on, it would be

_____

The best advice I've given
_____

_____

_____

_____

Proudest moment as a dad

_____

_____

_____

Some Favorites . . .

Foods _____

_____

Recreation _____

_____

Weekends _____

_____

_____

_____

Movie _____

_____

_____

Books _____

_____

_____

Heroes

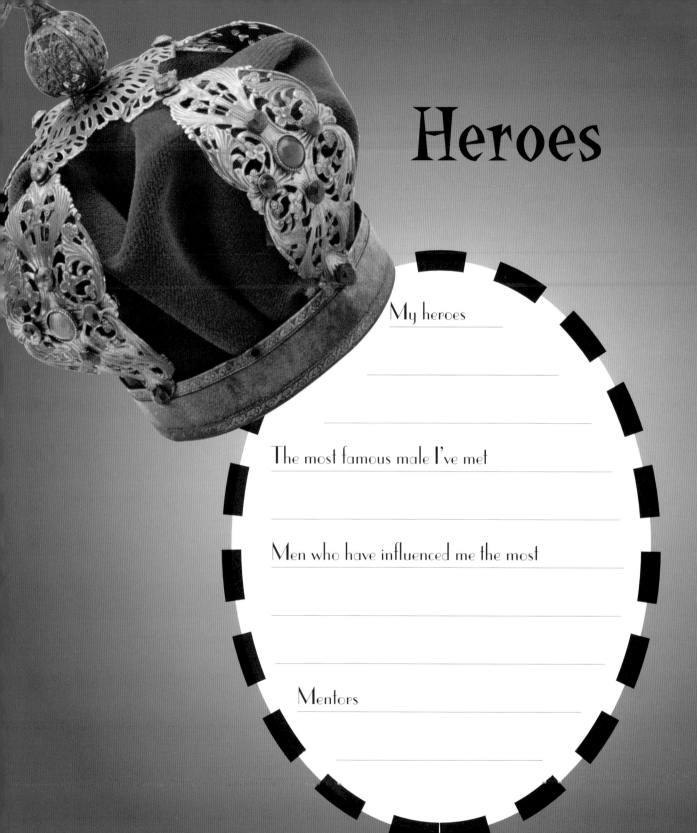

My heroes

_____

_____

The most famous male I've met

_____

Men who have influenced me the most

_____

_____

Mentors

_____

_____

Heroines

My heroines

_____

_____

The most famous female I've met

_____

Women who have influenced me the most

_____

_____

Mentors

_____

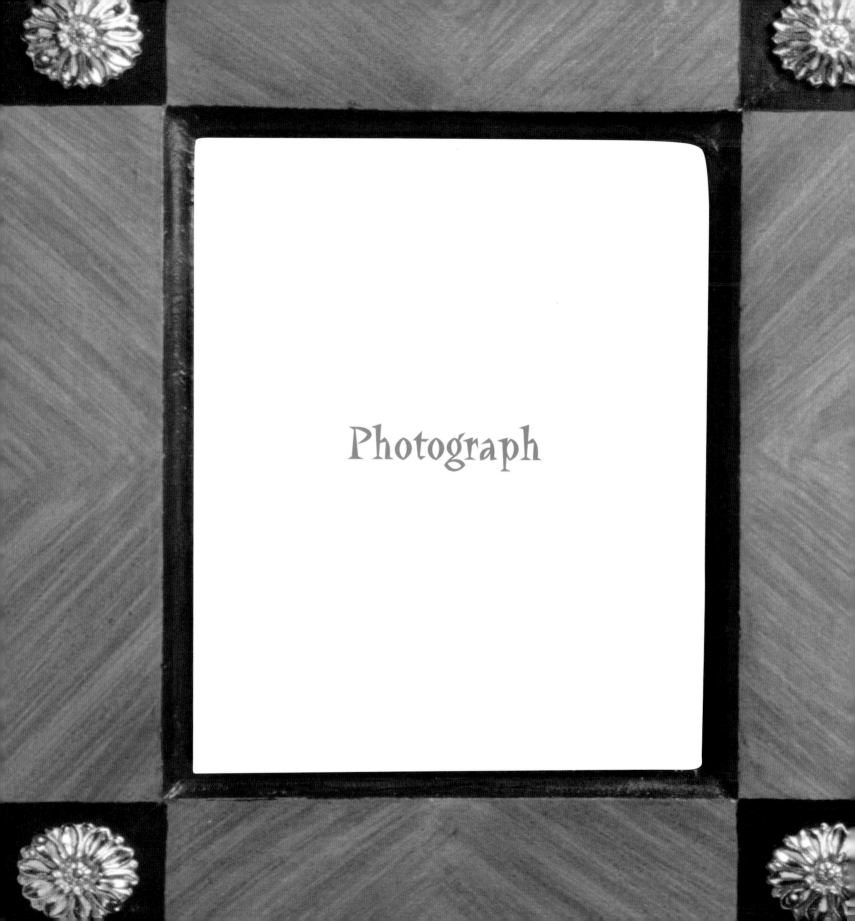

Photograph

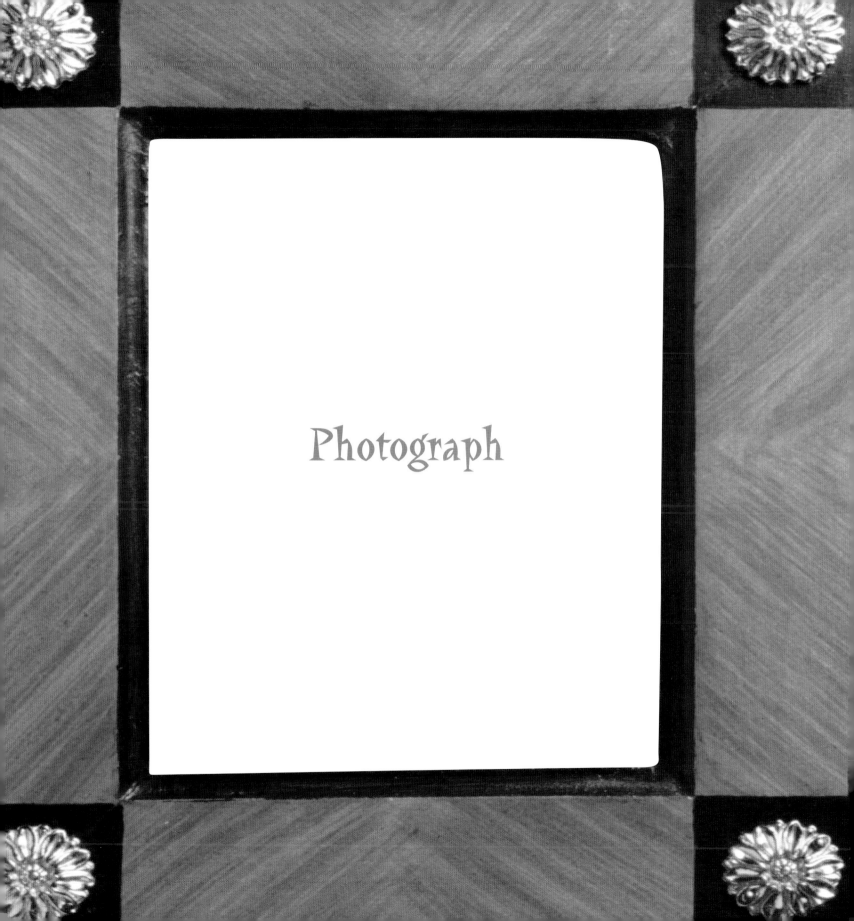

16

My plans

13

What I wish for you

14

Aspirations

15

Predictions

12

Expectations

Looking to the Future

Available Record Books
from Havoc

Baby

Coach

College Life

Couples

Dad

Girlfriends

Golf

Grandmother

Grandparents

Mom

Mothers & Daughters

My Pregnancy

Our Honeymoon

Retirement

School Days

Single Life

Sisters

Teacher

Traveling Adventures

Tying The Knot

Please write to us with your ideas for additional
Havoc Publishing Record Books and Products

HAVOC PUBLISHING
6330 Nancy Ridge Drive, Suite 104
San Diego, California 92121